I Am Climbing

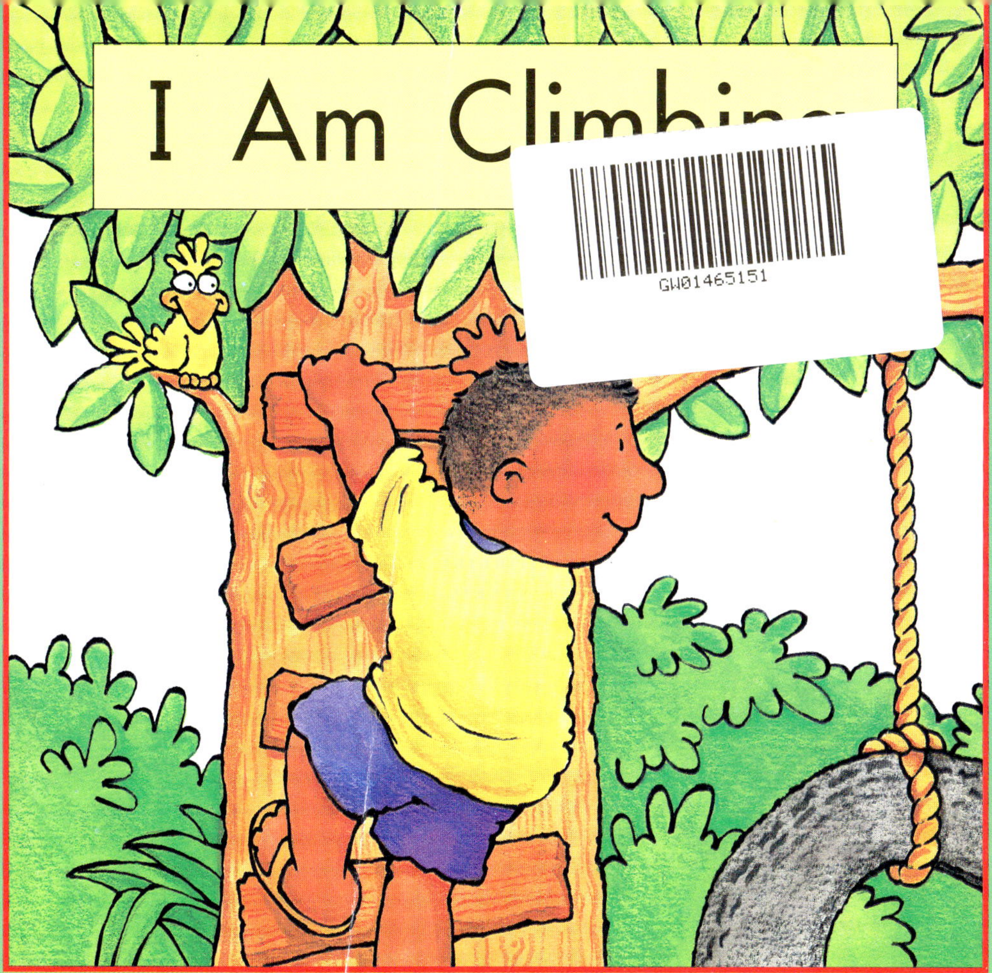

GW01465151

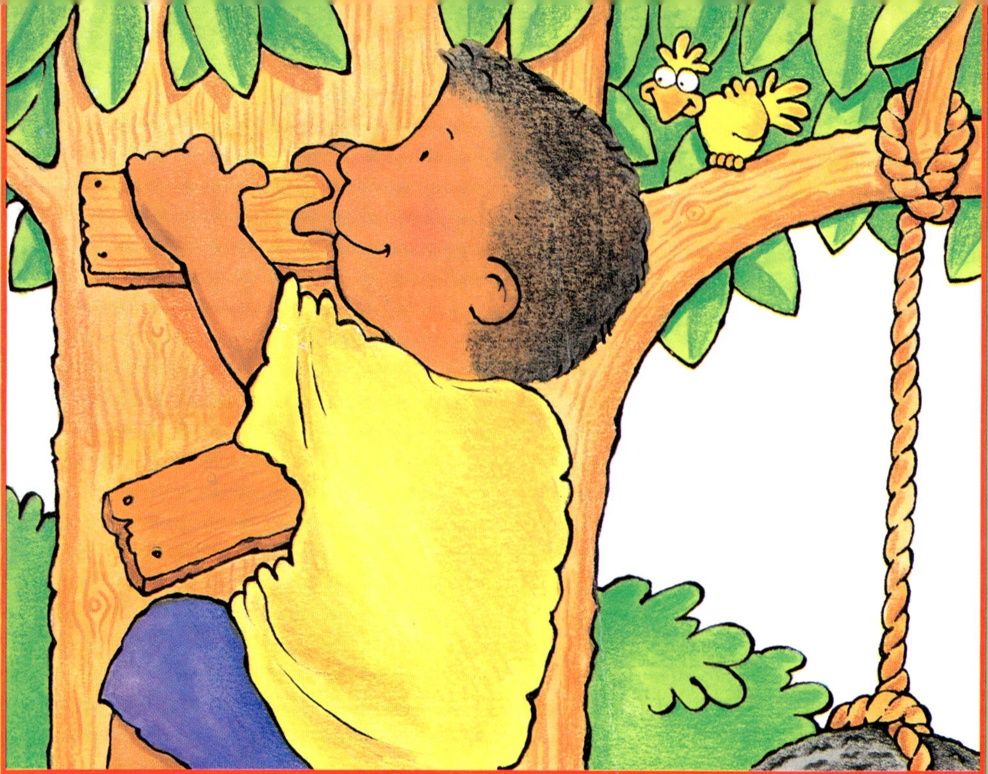

I am climbing.

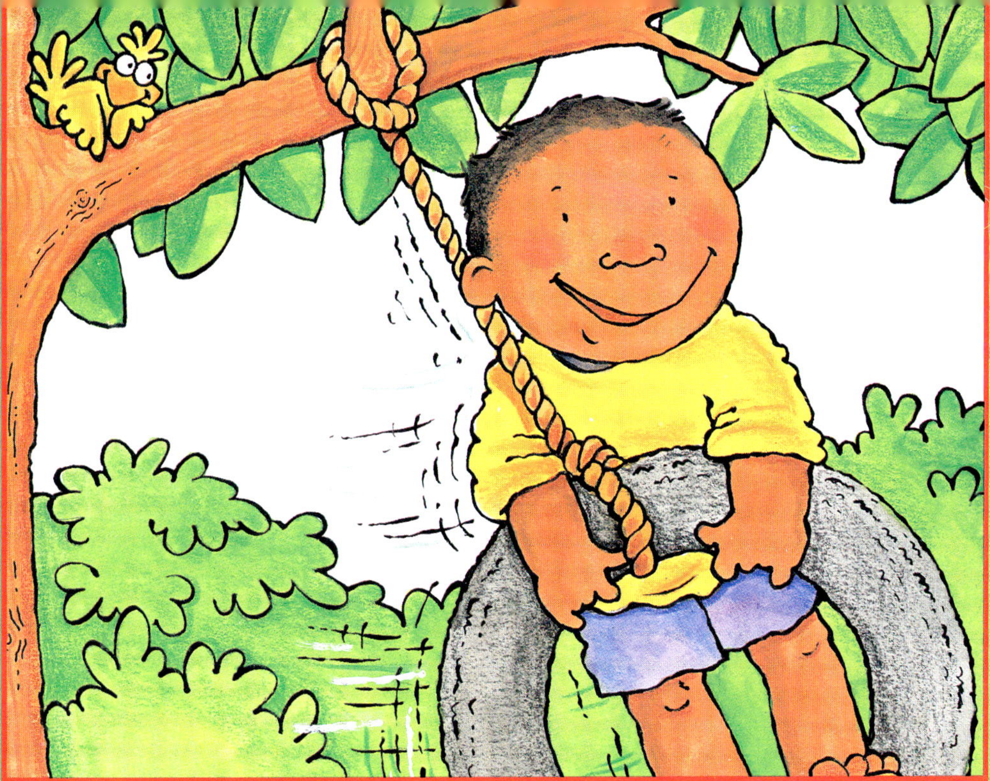

I am swinging.

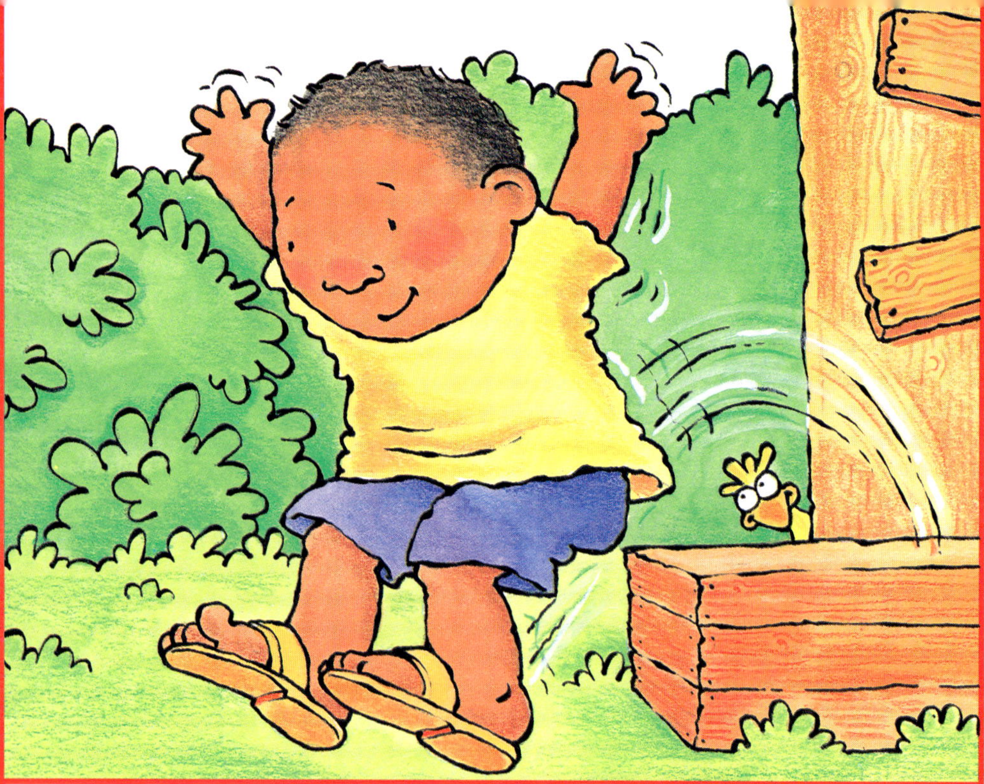

I am jumping.

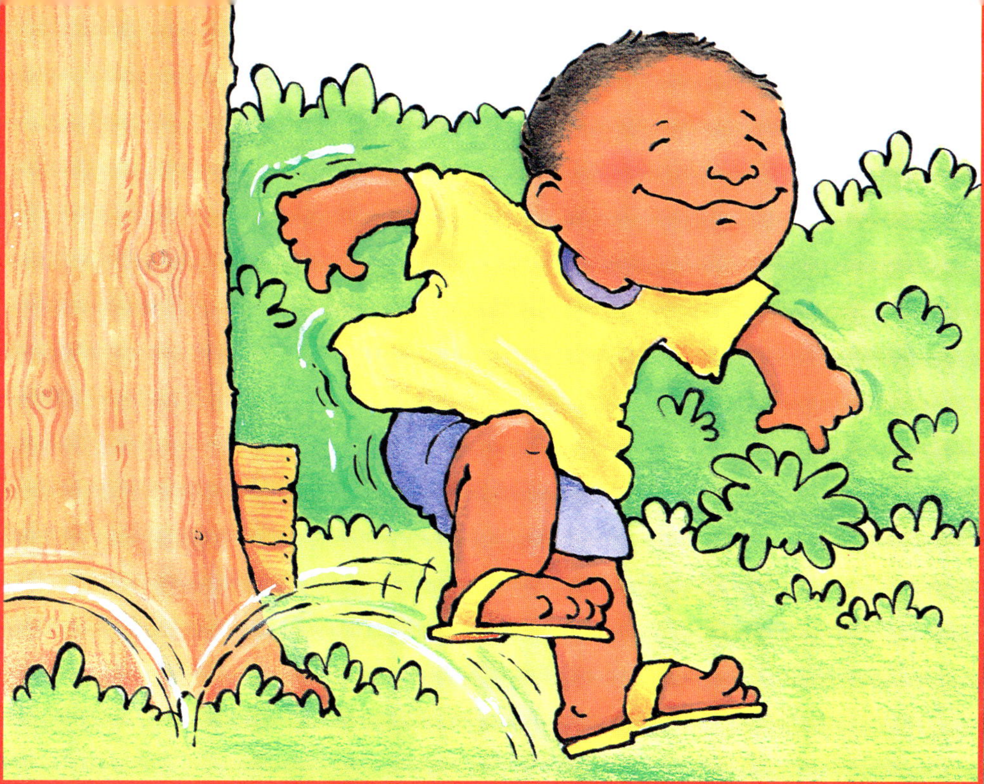

I am hopping.

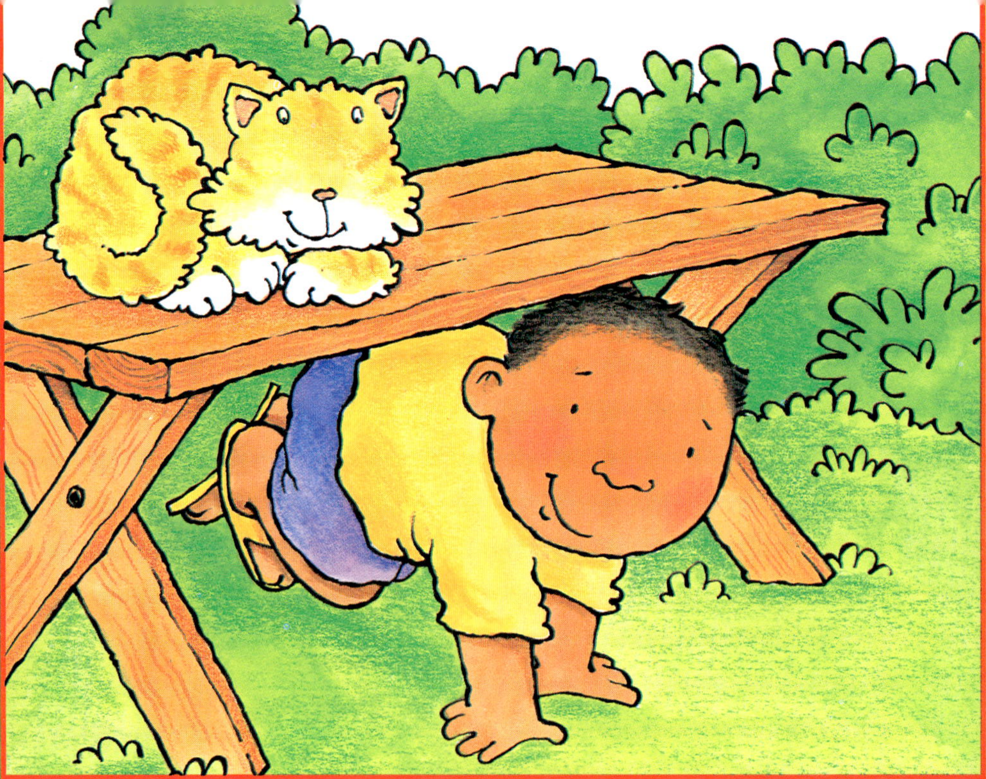

I am crawling.

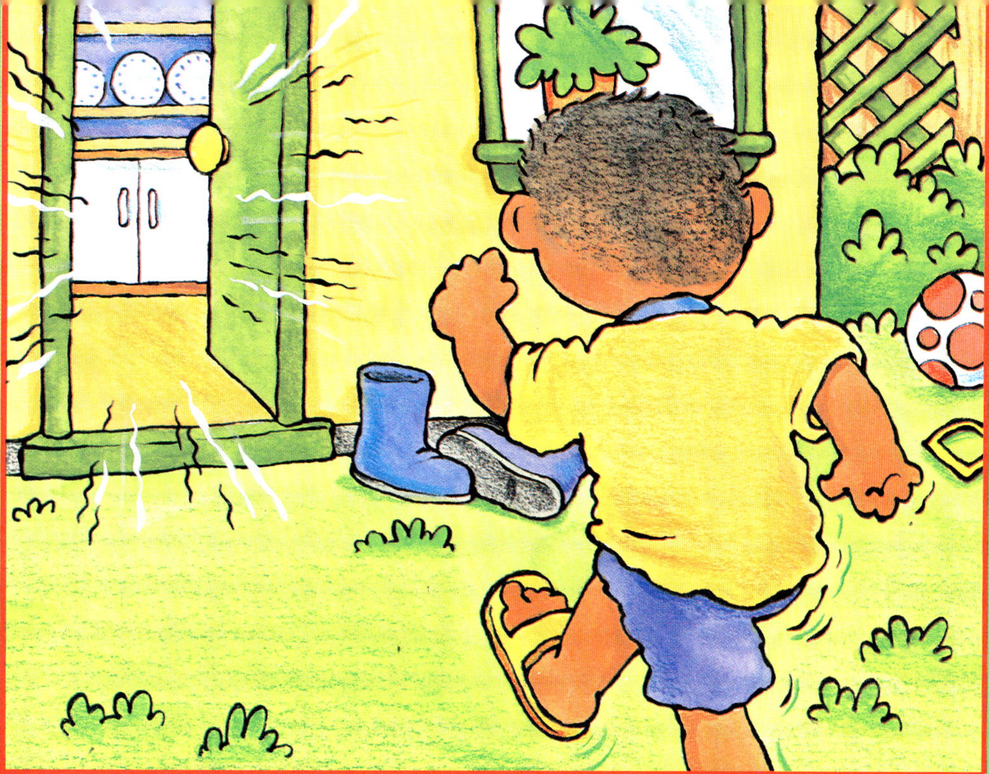

I am running...

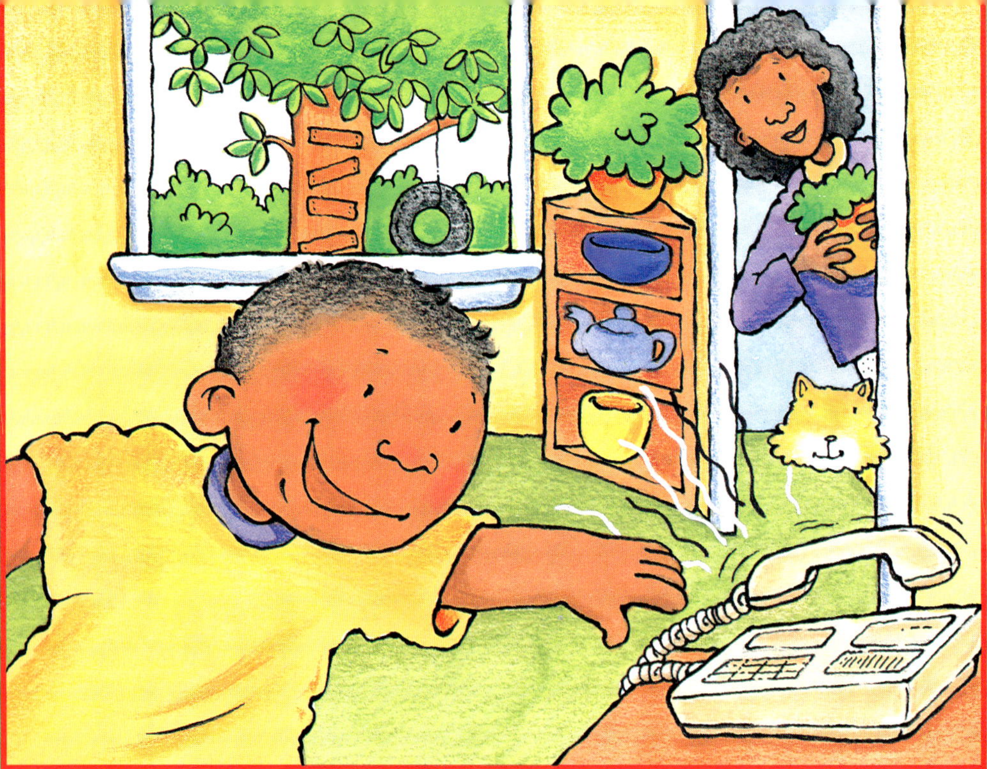

the phone is ringing!